Morinville Public Library

Dude, where's your helmet?

By David A. Duncan

RMB
Victoria Vancouver Calgary

For **Saul**

← This is Dan.

Many of Dan's friends call him "Mountain Man Dan," because he likes to do many outdoor activities.

One day, Mountain Man Dan decided to go rock climbing with his friend Vanessa. Dan woke up early the next day and got all of his rock climbing gear together.

When Dan met Vanessa, Dan noticed she was missing an important piece of equipment. Dan said...

"Dude, where's

your helmet?"

Vanessa replied...
"I don't want to wear my helmet, it's too heavy!"

So off they went.

Vanessa climbed first.

She climbed high up a rock face.

She climbed higher and higher.

Suddenly, a loose rock fell from the top of the cliff and **hit** Vanessa right on top of her head.

Vanessa **cried** in pain!

Dan had to rush Vanessa to the hospital. Doctor Lindy patched up Vanessa's head and gave her some medicine for the pain.

Then Doctor Lindy said...
"No more rock climbing for you!"

Vanessa was very sad.

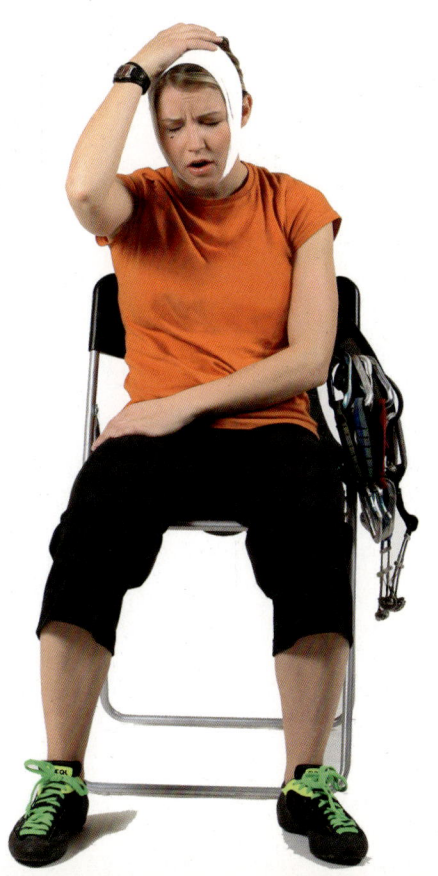

A few days later, Dan was feeling bored because he had nobody to go rock climbing with, so he decided to go mountain biking with his friend Jack. Dan woke up early the next morning and got all of his gear together.

When Dan met Jack he saw that Jack had **forgotten** something important. Dan asked... "**Dude, where's** Jack replied... "My head gets

your helmet?"

too **hot**. I don't need my helmet!"
So off they went mountain biking.

Dan and Jack were having fun riding down... down... down the mountain. Then all of a sudden Jack hit a rock and went flying over his handle bars.

He crashed **headfirst** into the ground. Jack hurt his head badly, so Dan rushed Jack to the **hospital**.

Doctor Lindy patched up Jack and then said firmly... "No more mountain

biking for you!"
Jack loved mountain biking
so he was very sad.

A little while later, Dan found himself **bored** again because he had **nobody** to rock climb or mountain bike with. **Winter** came, so Dan decided to go skiing with his snowboard buddy **Ben.** Dan woke up early the next morning and got all of his ski gear together.

your helmet?"

"Oh, I lost it. Besides, the snow is very soft. I'll be fine!"

So off they went.

Dan and Ben skied from the **top** of a mountain. They rode down... down... down.

They were having a **great** time until Ben lost his balance and rode into a tree **headfirst**.

Ben knocked his head **badly** so Dan took Ben to the hospital.

Doctor Lindy had to do some x-rays of Ben's head to make sure he didn't crack his skull. Then she wrapped him up and ordered Dan to take Ben home to rest. Before they left, Doctor Lindy said in an angry voice... "more snowboarding for you!"

Ben was very sad!

Several days later, Dan was feeling bored again because he had nobody to ski, rock climb or mountain bike with.

Dan decided to call his friend Dave to see if he wanted to go ice climbing with him.

The next morning, Dan woke up early and got all of his gear together.

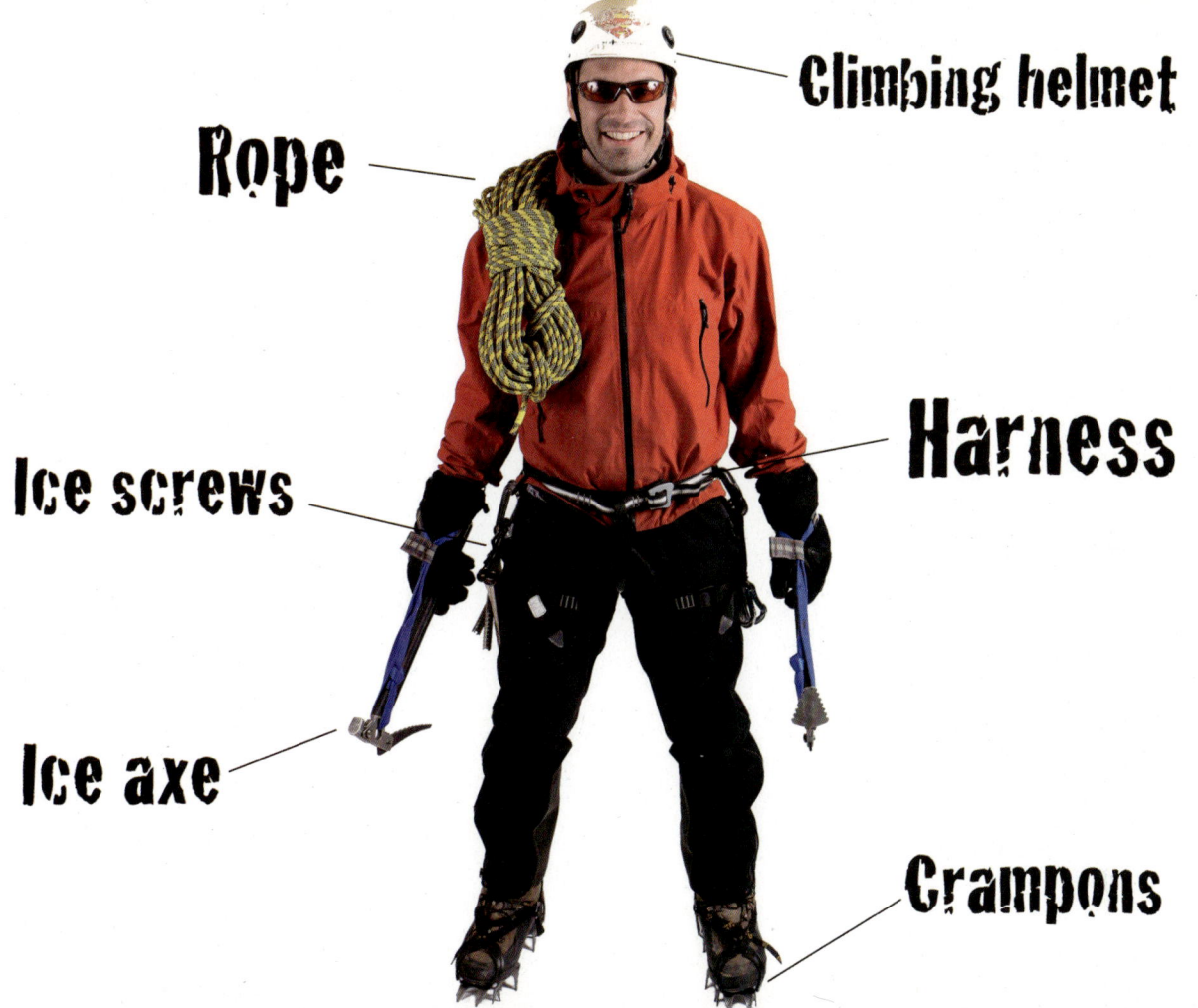

helmet?"

Dave replied... "It's somewhere in my basement, packed away. I don't need it today!"

So off they went ice-climbing.

Dan and Dave started to climb a huge frozen waterfall. It was a sunny day and it started to get warm outside.

Dave was **leading** the climb when all of a sudden a large icicle fell from above and broke over Dave's head. Dave was really **hurt,** so Dan had to rush him to the hospital.

When they got to the hospital, Doctor Lindy saw them coming and **shook** her head in **disappointment.** Doctor Lindy gave Dave a few stitches in his head because the ice had cut him. After Doctor Lindy patched him up, she **yelled** at him... "No more

ice climbing for you!"

Then Doctor Lindy turned to Dan and said...
"I don't want to see you bringing your friends here **again**, so be careful!"

Two weeks later, Dan was feeling bored again. He had nobody to rock climb, ski, mountain bike or ice climb with.

So Dan decided to go **caving** with his friend Allison.

Dan woke up early the next morning and got all of his gear together.

Dan was about to leave when he had an **idea**...

"Why don't I call Allison and remind her to bring her helmet?"

When Dan met Allison, he looked at her and said...

"Dude, where's Then Allison

your helmet?"

eached into her pack and pulled out a caving helmet with a headlamp.

Dan smiled and off they went caving.

Dan and Allison crawled deep... deep... deep... down into the earth.

As they were having fun caving, Allison did not realize the cave was getting smaller. Suddenly, she lifted her head and hit it on the roof of the cave.

Doctor Lindy Says...
"Remember to wear your

Copyright © 2009 David A. Duncan

All rights reserved. No part of this publication may be reproduced, stored in a retrieval system, or transmitted in any form or by any means—electronic, mechanical, audio recording, or otherwise—without the written permission of the publisher or a photocopying licence from Access Copyright, Toronto, Canada.

Rocky Mountain Books
#108 – 17665 66A Avenue
Surrey, BC V3S 2A7
www.rmbooks.com

Rocky Mountain Books
PO Box 468
Custer, WA
98240-0468

Library and Archives Canada Cataloguing in Publication

Duncan, David A.
Dude, where's your helmet? / David A. Duncan.

ISBN 978-1-897522-59-2

1. Helmets—Juvenile literature. 2. Sports—Safety measures—Juvenile literature. I. Title.

GV191.625.D85 2009   j796.028'9   C2009-903724-6

Printed in China

Rocky Mountain Books acknowledges the financial support for its publishing program from the Government of Canada through the Book Publishing Industry Development Program (BPIDP), Canada Council for the Arts, and the province of British Columbia through the British Columbia Arts Council and the Book Publishing Tax Credit.

This book has been produced on 100% post-consumer recycled paper, processed chlorine free and printed with Japanese soy-based dyes.